Philip Ardagh's Shortcuts

A FAST
AND FUNNY
GUIDE TO

Julius
Caesar

Philip Ardagh's Shortcuts

Elizabeth I

Florence Nightingale

Henry VIII

Julius Caesar

Marie Curie

Mary, Queen of Scots

Napoleon

Oliver Cromwell

Queen Victoria

William the Conqueror

Philip Ardagh's Shortcuts

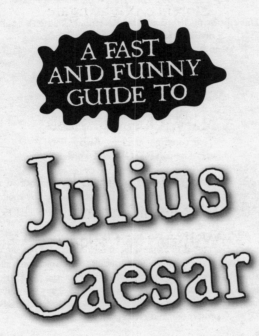

A FAST AND FUNNY GUIDE TO

Julius Caesar

Illustrated by Mike Phillips

MACMILLAN CHILDREN'S BOOKS

*For Ben Lynn, because I didn't get
to write to him when I was writing this*

First published 1999 by Macmillan Children's Books

This edition published 2013 by Macmillan Children's Books
a division of Macmillan Publishers Limited
20 New Wharf Road, London N1 9RR
Basingstoke and Oxford
Associated companies throughout the world
www.panmacmillan.com

ISBN 978-1-4472-4027-3

Text copyright © Philip Ardagh 1999
Illustrations copyright © Mike Phillips 1999

1 3 5 7 9 8 6 4 2

A CIP catalogue record for this book is available from the British Library.

Printed and bound by CPI Group (UK) Ltd, Croydon CR0 4YY

CONTENTS

The Roman empire (with a small 'e')
AT THE TIME OF CAESAR'S DEATH IN 44BC

Black Sea

BITHYNIA-PONTUS

Known as 'ASIA MINOR'

MACEDONIA

ASIA

CILICIA

Aegean sea

RHODES

CYPRUS

SYRIA

CRETE

CYRENE

ALEXANDRIA

USEFUL WORDS

. . . that you might come across if you don't just look at the funny pictures.

BC 'Before Christ'. These initials appear after all the dates in this book. These dates were not used in Caesar's time, because no one knew if or when Christ was going to be born! The smaller the number, the more recent the date.

Consul The top job in Rome. Two consuls were usually elected to rule side by side for a year, by the Senate.

Dictator An emergency ruler, with extra powers, elected by the Senate in times of crisis.

Eagle Each legion had a carved silver eagle, mounted on a standard, and carried into battle to symbolize the legion's power. If the eagle (called an *aquila*) was lost to the enemy, the legion was disbanded.

Forum An open space at the centre of Rome (and other Roman towns too). A place to shop, but also to meet and talk and discuss politics.

Legion A unit of soldiers. By Caesar's day, it was made up of about 5,000 soldiers.

Patrician The highest class of Roman citizen. Originally, only patricians could be elected to the Senate.

Quaestor A government official. Twenty were chosen a year.

Romulus and Remus Legendary twins brought up by a she-wolf. As adults, Romulus is supposed to have killed Remus, built the city of Rome and been its first ruler.

Senate 600 or so senators elected from all classes of citizen to rule Rome on their behalf. Fat chance!

LITTLE CAESAR

When writing about someone who lived such a very
long time ago, nothing's straightforward. Take Julius
Caesar's birthday, for a start – which is a good place
to start in a book about Caesar's life. It's generally accepted
that Julius Caesar was born on 12 *Quintilis* 100 BC. (The
month *Quintilis* was later renamed July after him, by a chap
named Mark Antony.) But how do we know? Brainy people
have agreed that this was his date of birth because it's
known he was born on a 12 July, and the 100 BC comes from
the fact that experts are pretty sure that Caesar was in his
56th year when he died in March 44 BC.

Because BC dates work backwards, simply add 56 years to 44 years BC and you get the date 100 BC . . . though there are some who argue that he might actually have been born in 102 BC! Ho hum. Back to the drawing board. This is when a little 'c' – like this one: *c.* – comes in handy.

WHAT CIRCA IS ABOUT

When historians write down a date they're not 100 per cent sure about, and they don't want you chasing after them shouting 'Prove it!' or, even worse, 'Liar!', they often put the magic '*c.*' in front of it. This is short for the Latin word *circa* which means 'about'. In other words, 'Not sure, but around about then-ish'. So we can safely say that Julius Caesar was born 'round about 100 BC' or *c.*100 BC. That looks very professional now, doesn't it?

LATIN AND THE LATINS

Latin was the language of Romans. The original Romans came from a tribe called the Latins, which is how the language got its name. A Roman originally meant someone from the city of Rome – formed when seven settlements grew into one big one. Later, when the people of Rome created an empire (sometimes with a small 'e' and sometimes with a big 'E', but more on that later), Romans came from many different parts of it. The Romans occupied and ruled most of the countries in the known world.

MEET THE FAMILY

Julius Caesar, called *Gaius* Julius Caesar by his parents, was the only son of another Gaius Julius Caesar (Dad) and Aurelia (Mum). His dad had been a praetor (government official) and his mum came from an aristocratic family. They certainly had money – they were probably quite rich, in fact – but the Caesars led strict simple lives. Mr and Mrs Caesar weren't into the latest fashions unlike many of the other wealthy Romans of the time. Julius Caesar's uncle was a man named Gaius Marius – Uncle Marius for short – who was consul. This was a top job. Each year, two consuls were elected to rule Rome.

THE MAKE-UP OF POWER

When Caesar was born, Rome was a republic, which means that it had no king or emperor but was governed by a group of senators in the Senate. Senators were elected by Roman citizens. Not everyone in Rome was a citizen. For a start, no women could be citizens and neither could very poor people or foreigners, to name but a few.

CAESAR'S CHILDHOOD

So what's known about Julius Caesar's early childhood? The answer can be spelled out in two words: v-e-r-y l-i-t-t-l-e! What we *do* know is that he was taught Greek by a man called Antonius Gnipho who was a Gaul from what's now

12

northern Italy. (The tribes of Gauls occupied much of what we now call France, and land as far north as the Rhine and as far south as the Italian Alps.) We also know that the young Caesar wrote a poem in honour of the Roman hero Hercules.

SNAFFLED FROM THE GREEKS

It was important for educated Romans to read Ancient Greek, because that's where they stole – er, sorry, I meant to say *developed* – so many of their ideas from. Take, for example, the well-known Roman legend of 'The Twelve Labours of Hercules'. This was suspiciously like an earlier Greek legend of 'The Twelve Labours of Heracles' . . . Well, EXACTLY like the earlier Greek legend of 'The Twelve Labours of Heracles', except that the Romans changed his name from Heracles to Hercules. The truth be told, most Roman gods and goddesses were originally Ancient Greek gods and goddesses with a swift name-change!

WHY WOULD A ROMAN WANT TO EAT A GREEK SALAD?

WHICH IS WHY I'M GOING TO CALL IT A CAESAR SALAD, INSTEAD!

VEGE WHATSIT?

Although there are no photographs – remember, we're talking about over 2,000 years ago here – no pictures and no carvings of the young Julius Caesar, we do have a description of what he looked like, written by a Roman historian about 150 years later. According to this, he had neat hair, a big nose, full lips and *nigris vegetisque oculis*, which is Latin for 'dark, piercing eyes'. We're also told that he fastened his girdle in such an odd, loose way that it attracted attention!!!

TOGA! TOGA! TOGA!

What you could wear depended on WHO you were. Just by looking at a Roman's clothes, you would have been able to tell a great deal about how important they were . . . or weren't, as the case may be. This wasn't a matter of designer labels. There was a strict dress code.

Only citizens could wear togas, for starters, and only senators could wear them with purple edges. Poorer people went around in tunics. A tunic was a bit like a giant T-shirt with a cord around the middle.

MARKED OUT FOR BIG THINGS

When Caesar was about fourteen, his Uncle Marius – still the most important person in Rome – made him a Priest of Jupiter and a member of the Sacred College. This was not only a great honour, but also came with a handsome income – in other words, he was paid good money for it. Unfortunately, Uncle Marius's days were numbered. After being exiled to Africa, he returned to Rome in 86 BC, wiped out his enemies and was elected consul for an amazing seventh time, only to drop dead a few days later.

A BRIEF ENGAGEMENT . . .

Before Julius was even sixteen, the other Gaius Julius (his dad) arranged for him to become engaged to be married to a woman named Cossutia, but the young Caesar had other ideas. Luckily for him – if that's the right way of looking at it – his dad died in 84 BC. The death was sudden and unexpected and happened in Pisa, which is more famous today for its leaning tower. With his father gone, Caesar quickly broke off the engagement.

. . . ANOTHER WOMAN

And, just as quickly, he married someone else: a woman called Cornelia. Now it is, of course, possible that Julius

Caesar married Cornelia because he thought that she was the most wonderful person in the world and that he had lovey-dovey feelings about her every time anyone even mentioned her name. What's far more likely is that he married her because she was the daughter of Cinna. And who was Cinna?

Well, not long after Uncle Marius stopped being the most important person in all of Rome, Cinna took his place. He was consul now . . . and Caesar was married to his daughter.

It seems more than very likely that this boy had some very big ideas up his sleeve (not that a toga has sleeves, of course). There is another reason why Julius Caesar might have married Cornelia so quickly, though. She was going to have their baby. They called her Julia.

16

A WHOLE LOT OF JULIES

The reason why Caesar and his dad were called 'Julius' and his aunt was called 'Julia', and now so was his daughter, was because Caesar came from a family, or clan, called 'Gens Julia' or 'Julii', so variations on the name were passed on from generation to generation. So now you know.

POPULARIS AND OPTIMATES

Both Caesar's Uncle Marius and his wife's father Cinna were members of the 'popular' party in Roman politics and government. Members of the *popularis* (that's Latin) had the laws they wanted passed agreed to by a people's assembly – so they were popular with ordinary citizens. Another powerful group of Roman politicians at the time were called the *optimates* (which is Latin too). *Optimates* were the rich upper classes – the aristocracy of Ancient Rome – who wanted all the laws agreed to by the Senate, without having to answer to the people! They thought that the *popularis* were revolutionaries, with dangerous new-fangled ideas.

AN ILL WIND

Julius Caesar's world was turned upside down when he was eighteen years old. His father and his influential Uncle Marius were both already dead, his father-in-law – Cornelia's dad, Cinna – had been killed by his own men in a mutiny, and Marius's old enemy, Sulla (sometimes spelled Sylla) – one of the *optimates* – crushed the populist forces in Rome in 82 BC. Sulla made himself dictator and over 4,000 Romans were killed in the terrors that followed.

NOT A MARIUS FAN

Usually, Roman dictators were only appointed by the Senate in times of extreme crisis, such as war, but Sulla used his powers to weaken the people's assembly and the populists. He also gave more power to his supporters, the aristocrats. Sulla hated the most successful populist – Caesar's Uncle Marius – even though he was dead! He ordered all statues of Marius to be pulled down, and had the dead man's ashes thrown in the River Tiber!

18

A POWERFUL ENEMY

Sulla could easily have had Julius Caesar killed, but obviously saw something remarkable in the young man. He told Julius to divorce Cornelia, to break any connections with his populist past, and to marry a woman of his – Sulla's that is – choosing. Caesar refused outright, which was a very risky thing to do . . . but Sulla wasn't so quick to give up.

NO JOB, NO INHERITANCE, NO WAY

Sulla stripped young Caesar of his title as Priest of Jupiter and of the money that went with it. To make matters worse, he took away the dowry that Cinna had given Caesar when he'd married his daughter. If that wasn't enough, Sulla also confiscated all the land and property Caesar had inherited from his father when he'd died. But still Caesar refused to divorce Cornelia . . . which some people thought was rather foolish.

19

A PRICE ON HIS HEAD

Sulla had had enough. He had hoped that Julius Caesar would be a part of his plans, but now the young man was a problem. Sulla didn't like problems. He liked solutions, so he offered assassins money to kill Caesar. As soon as he heard the news, Caesar went into hiding but was quickly discovered. He managed to escape by bribing the right people.

Meanwhile, Caesar's powerful friends and relations did all they could to earn him a pardon. These included an organization called the College of the Vestal Virgins and Mamercus Aemilius, a highly respected patrician.

LOOK, I HOPE YOU DON'T THINK I'M TRYING TO BRIBE YOU...BUT WOULD YOU LOOK AFTER THIS GOLD FOR ME?

YOU HAVE BEEN WARNED

Sulla finally agreed to spare Caesar's life but, according to the Roman historian Suetonius – whom most brainy scholars think told less fibs than other, later Roman biographers of Caesar – he gave this warning: 'The youth . . . will, one day, overthrow the aristocracy for whom you and I have fought so hard. In this young Caesar there are many Mariuses.' In other words, if you thought that his Uncle Marius, the populist, was a problem, just wait and see what this boy does.

CAESAR:
SOLDIER AND SPEECHMAKER

Despite the pardon, Julius Caesar was wise enough to put a good distance between himself and Sulla, just in case the dictator changed his mind. He became a soldier abroad. In 80 BC, he served under Thermus (which sounds like something to keep your coffee hot, but was, in fact, the name of a praetor). Thermus's job was to suppress ship-loads of pirates who were making waves in the Aegean Sea. When I say 'making waves', I mean 'causing trouble' not literally making waves in the Aegean Sea, though they probably did.

L-L-LET ME GUESS. YOU'RE A P- P- P- PIRATE, RIGHT?

OUR MAN IN BITHYNIA

Thermus didn't have a big enough fleet to defeat the pirates, so wanted to borrow some ships from the nearby kingdom of Bithynia. Not long after Caesar arrived from Rome, Thermus sent him to Bithynia's royal court to negotiate with King Nicomedes. Years later, Julius Caesar's enemies tried to make out that he was too friendly with this foreign king, but there is no real evidence to support this.

MILITARY HONOURS

Caesar, who was now twenty (100 BC – 80 BC = 20 years), returned to Thermus with the ships the Roman forces needed. He then went on to win the *corona civica* or 'oak leaf' which was the second highest military decoration there was, and a very great honour. He was awarded it for the part he played in the storming of the city of Mytilene. Unfortunately, we're not sure what dashing deeds he performed, but the *corona civica* was awarded to people who saved the lives of fellow soldiers, so he was obviously a bit of a hero.

PIRATICAL PROBLEMS

Caesar wasn't so successful serving under Servilius Isauricus, whose name sounds less like a thermos flask and more like a small dinosaur. Isauricus's orders were to defeat the pirate hordes who were dodging their would-be captors by hiding out in the many creeks and rivers in Cilicia . . . The Roman forces seem to be getting nowhere so when, in 78 BC, Caesar learnt of the death of Sulla – who'd given up his dictatorship and retired in 79 BC – he decided to go back to Rome.

SPEECH! SPEECH!

Well educated men from well-to-do backgrounds, such as Caesar, often became orators. These were public speakers who put forward a point of view, explained a cause or even acted like lawyers in trials, defending or prosecuting. Caesar hadn't been back in Rome long when he had a chance to put his oratory skills to the test.

He acted as prosecutor in the trial of Gnaeus Cornelius Dolabella, a friend and supporter of his old enemy Sulla. Dolabella was, in turn, supported by the Senate and provided with the best advocate of the day, Aurelius Cotta. Cotta was far more skilled and practised than Julius Caesar, and Dolabella walked free. But it had been an important trial and it had got Caesar in the public eye yet again.

A MAN OF MEANS ONCE MORE

In the meantime, Caesar had used his friends and influence to get back all the property Sulla had taken away from him, and was even a Priest of Jupiter once more. He had money and time on his hands, and decided to use some of that time brushing up his orating at a school in Rhodes, run by the (then) famous orator Apollonius Molon. On his way to Rhodes, though, Julius Caesar had an awfully big adventure . . .

PRISONER OF THE PIRATES

The ship carrying Caesar and his servants and slaves to Rhodes was boarded and seized in the Aegean Sea by a band of pirates. The pirates took Caesar and three of his attendants to an island called Pharmacusa, off the Carian coast, and held him hostage. What they wanted was money, so they let the others go to try to raise a ransom.

HIGHER! HIGHER!

One version of events says that when Caesar learnt that his ransom was to be 20 talents (quite a lot), he flew into a rage and said that he was worth 50 talents (a lot)! He spent six weeks with the pirates and they treated him well. He wrote poetry, joined in their sports and games and was as polite to them as they were to him . . . but he did point out that he'd be back to make sure that they were all executed for their crimes.

CRUCIFIED!

Finally, the ransom was paid and Julius Caesar was put ashore on the mainland near Miletus. As soon as he was on dry land, he got together a force of men and sailed straight back to the pirates' island. His captors were still sharing the money between them, when Caesar's men captured each and every one of them. The pirates were taken to a place called Pergamus, where they were found guilty and sentenced to be crucified. Crucifixion – being nailed to a wooden cross – was a slow and painful death and, despite having been their prisoner, Caesar pleaded that their executions be quicker . . . so the pirates were strangled before being put on the crosses, which was still not the nicest way to go. Caesar was now ready to finish his journey to Rhodes to improve his public speaking.

THE PROBLEM WITH PIRATES

Pirates were a really big headache for the Romans at that time. The Romans were a powerful force and conquered many neighbouring countries, but they certainly didn't rule the waves. The pirates became really well organized, basing themselves in Cilicia, with plenty of trees to cut down and turn into pirate ships. At one stage, there were over a thousand well-armed pirate vessels, divided into pirate squadrons under pirate commanders! They spent some of their plunder on bribing the Roman aristocracy to make sure that the Senate left them alone.

TROUBLE BREWS

Everyone knew that the government of Rome was now corrupt, and that those who disagreed with it often ended up dead. People lived in fear, not knowing what might happen next, and there were grumblings of revolution in the air. (Sounds dramatic, huh?) Mithridates, King of Pontus (which was allowed some independence under Roman rule in Asia Minor), had always spelled trouble for his Roman masters. In one rebellion led by him in the past, over 150,000 people were said to have died in one day. Although this is probably a whopping great exaggeration, it suggests that a lot of people did die. Sulla had defeated him then, but Sulla was dead and Mithridates was ready to try to push the Romans out of Asia Minor in what became known as the Third Mithridatic War.

ASIA MINOR

Asia Minor was certainly one of Rome's wealthiest provinces, if not *the* most wealthy, and that wealth poured into Rome . . . at least, it should have. Now the Romans were in danger of the province breaking free of Rome. The Roman governors in charge of the region were more interested in making themselves richer, and the Roman generals were more interested in what was good for them than in what was good for Rome. The region was ripe for rebellion.

CAESAR TO THE RESCUE

Meanwhile, back in Rhodes, Julius Caesar heard what was going on and didn't like the sound of it. He couldn't sit around being taught by Apollonius all day when there was important work to be done! So he travelled to Asia, raised a raggle-taggle army of willing volunteers, then faced King Mithridates's generals and defeated them. There was one teeny-weeny problem with this. Because Caesar wasn't an official soldier, just an ordinary private citizen, it was against the law for him to raise an army and lead it into battle . . . Luckily for him, no one seemed to mind!

BACK HOME

The year 69 BC saw Julius Caesar back in Rome, now aged thirty-one, which isn't that old, honestly. Ask your gran. He was living with his wife and daughter, and his mother Aurelia. It was well known that he'd been an enemy of the hated Sulla and had served Rome well in Asia so he was very popular with ordinary citizens. He was elected Military Tribune, and helped recreate the People's Assembly which had been banned by Sulla and his *optimates*.

CAESAR IN THE SENATE

A year later, Caesar was elected quaestor, which gave him a place in the Senate and made him very happy. What made him less happy was the death of his Aunt Julia, who had been married to Uncle Marius. At her funeral, Caesar gave a speech in which he praised Marius and Cinna and made it clear that he too supported the *popularis*. He was quickly gaining a reputation as a man of the people.

DEATH AND SADNESS

In that same year (68 BC), Caesar's wife, Cornelia, died and – very unusually for the time – Caesar held a *laudatio* (which means 'funeral eulogy' . . . which means 'speech for the dead person') for her. Caesar married a second time. His new wife, Pompeia, was the cousin of a famous Roman soldier and politician named Pompey. It was Pompey's military campaigns that had made Asia Minor Roman territory, and he also suppressed the slave rebellion led by a slave named Spartacus. Probably as a result of Pompey's insistence, Caesar was then sent to Spain to help sort out the financial mess in this troubled province.

SO LITTLE DONE . . .

It was in Spain that, according to the writer Plutarch, Julius Caesar saw the statue of the great warrior Alexander the Great and burst into tears. When his friends asked him why he was crying, he said: 'At my age, Alexander had conquered so many nations and, in all this time, I've done nothing memorable!'

ON THE UP AND UP

After leaving Spain and returning to Rome, Caesar was appointed an aedile. Though the job itself wasn't important – you even had to pay your own expenses! – it was an important *stepping stone*. Anyone who wanted the chance to be elected to the top job of consul one day, had to be an aedile along the way. The aediles were in charge of the public buildings and the games of ancient Rome, and had to decorate the city and put on spectacular events to wow the masses.

I WAS EXPECTING MORE DRAMATIC DECORATIONS, THAT'S ALL... LEAPING STONE LIONS, SWOOPING EAGLES, THAT SORT OF THING...

FUN DAY AT THE LUDI

The three different types of public entertainment were called 'Ludi', which is Latin for 'the games'. These were chariot races (which were the most popular), the theatre, and gladiator fights and animal hunts.

In the days of the early Republic, all three events would take place on the same day in the same arena. Later, they took place on different days in their own purpose-built buildings. There was plenty of blood and guts at the gladiator fights and even the chariot races, which were very dangerous indeed.

BUILDING A REPUTATION

As an aedile, Caesar had a new temple built, added columns to the front of an important building and paid for some of the biggest and 'best' gladiator fights Rome had ever seen . . . if you like that sort of thing. (Caesar himself didn't like gladiator fights much, but he knew what *the people* liked and that was important to him.) Meanwhile, in the Senate, and in Rome's main meeting place, the Forum, Caesar continued to build his reputation as a brilliant and honest man who believed in the rights of ordinary people.

TOP PRIEST

Soon Julius Caesar had his eye on another important job. He wanted to be Pontifex Maximus, the chief priest. Now, there was the minor fact that he didn't believe in the Roman gods and goddesses and thought that they were just a bunch of made-up characters in stories, rather than living, breathing deities who should be worshipped . . . But why should that stop him being chief priest? He was already in debt for all the money he had to spend on being an aedile, but he spent more money on his campaign to be Pontifex Maximus. And, on 6 March 63 BC, he won. Caesar got

more votes than all the other candidates put together . . .
Not only that, he was chosen to be praetor for the following
year. And it was as praetor that the Senate turned against
him.

TROUBLE & SCANDAL (IN OPEN-TOED SANDALS)

A consul and top man in Rome at the time was a man called Cicero, who was becoming more stubborn and unpopular by the day. Many people wanted the famous general Pompey to return to Rome and take charge. He was always very popular with ordinary citizens, and his popularity grew once he'd finally sorted out all those troublesome pirates. The official who supported Pompey's cause (whilst he was away) was the tribune Metellus and, as praetor, Caesar supported Metellus.

A VILE TRIAL

A group of Roman traitors were found to be conspiring with the Gauls – the most dreaded enemies of Rome – and the suspects were put on trial. No one argued against this. You couldn't have people consorting with barbarians and planning to overthrow the state! The only trouble was that those accused of the crime weren't given a fair trial. In fact, they weren't even allowed to say a single word in their own defence. As praetor, Caesar didn't argue the men's innocence, he simply reasoned that things should be done properly. They weren't. Cicero wanted a swift execution, and the accused were strangled in their cells.

SHUT UP!

Cicero had done so many oh-so-nasty things during his time as consul, and that was just one example of them. On the last day of 62 BC, Cicero stood up in the Senate about to give a speech looking back on his time as consul, when Metellus told him to sit down and shut up. If Cicero hadn't allowed his prisoners to speak, Metellus argued, then Cicero himself shouldn't be allowed to speak! There was uproar.

NO, YOU SHUT UP!

A few days later, after Cicero had ranted and raved at Metellus until he was as purple as a beetroot, Metellus put forward a proposal to the people of Rome: that Pompey and his army should be recalled to the city to bring back law, order and dignity. Caesar supported Metellus in this, knowing that the whole system of government would fall apart round their ears if someone didn't take drastic action soon. Metellus then officially put forward his proposal at the Forum, only to have the scroll he was reading from snatched from his hand ... so he carried on speaking without it. Next, his enemies put their hands over his mouth and shut him up with brute force. Everyone was cleared out of the Forum.

CARRY ON REGARDLESS

Using powers that they didn't really have, the Senate (which, at that time was filled with aristocratic supporters of Cicero) stripped both Caesar and Metellus of their titles. While Metellus left Rome to travel to Asia to tell Pompey what was going on, Julius Caesar simply carried on life as normal. As far as he was concerned, the Senate had no power to stop him being praetor, so he simply carried on being praetor! This enraged the Senate who had his office closed, but he was surrounded by an enormous crowd of ordinary citizens who supported him. They accompanied him home (to the palace of the chief priest) and gathered outside there every day.

WITHIN THE LAW

As chief priest and head of the *popularis*, Caesar now had enormous support. The mob urged him to become their leader and to order them to pull down the Senate and throw the corrupt senators out onto the streets, but he resisted. He argued that it was far better for them to *obey* the law whilst everyone else was breaking it – to show that they were well and truly in the right. The Senate, meanwhile, was in a state of panic. Rome could have a revolution on its hands! Apologies were quickly sent to Caesar and he was asked to return to the Senate.

ARE YOU THE MOB?

NO, SORRY, WE'RE THE HUGE CROWD. THE MOB IS JUST AROUND THE CORNER

FRAMED!

Some of Caesar's worst enemies in the Senate were still out to get him, though, so they made up claims that he was behind some dastardly deeds against Rome. No one believed it and it was the accusers themselves who ended up being arrested . . . narrowly avoiding being torn limb from limb by an angry mob of Caesar's supporters. They probably felt a lot safer in jail!

WOMEN TROUBLE

One thing it was easy to 'accuse' Julius Caesar of was liking to be with women. While most Roman men loved watching gladiator fights and chariot races, Caesar much preferred spending his time away from these events . . . in the company of ladies. He became very popular with the wives and daughters of some very important citizens, and rumours started to spread. Pompey even heard reports that Caesar was spending rather too much time with his wife while he was off fighting abroad. The clever thing about such rumours is that it is very difficult to prove they aren't true, and Caesar was stuck with this reputation.

BRUTUS, MY BOY

One scandalous Roman rumour of the time was that Caesar was in love with a woman called Servilia, but the rumour didn't end there. It was said that Caesar was the father of Servilia's son, Brutus. This meant that Julius Caesar would have become a father when he was only about fifteen years old! There's no proof that this was more than a rumour, but it's an interesting one because of the important part Brutus played at the end of Caesar's life. (And, if you don't know what important part Brutus played at the end of Caesar's life – or should that be *in* the ending of Caesar's life – you'll just have to wait and see.) He grew up to be a famous soldier and a great believer in the rights of the people of the Republic of Rome.

WOMEN FOLK, BEYOND A JOKE

A popular new religion – the worshipping of the goddess the Bona Dea – was spreading across Rome and a festival was held in her honour once a year. This festival didn't take place at a temple, but in the house of an important official (a different one each year). When it was the Chief Priest's turn, Caesar wasn't actually there himself because it was a women-only festival. Caesar's second wife, Pompeia, was in charge of all the ceremonies. With Caesar out of the way, she invited her friend Clodius Puer (who was nicknamed 'Pretty Boy') to the festival, disguised as a woman!

UNDRESSED AND DISTRESSED

Clodius's disguise obviously wasn't a very good one. Angry guests, realizing that a man had snuck into their women-only festival, tore off his clothes, beat him up and threw him out! Reports of what had happened soon spread and Clodius was put on trial for his behaviour. Although the 'crime' wasn't that serious, there was no doubt that he'd be found guilty of it. But he wasn't.

With friends in high places, the judges were bribed to pronounce him innocent. This caused more of an outcry than the original offence! The corruption of Rome was there for all to see. Julius Caesar divorced Pompeia for her part in the affair. When asked why he'd thought this necessary, he simply replied: 'The wife of Caesar must be above suspicion.'

SPAIN AGAIN

Caesar actually went abroad before the trial was even under way. His period as praetor was at an end and he'd gone back to Spain. Here he quickly gained new territories for Rome, sent large sums of money to the Treasury, quashed the local bandits who roamed the countryside, and sorted out a few administrative problems (probably all before breakfast). The truth be told, he'd left for Spain before the appointment was even officially confirmed. This was because he was already in debt again, and wanted to leave town – that should be *city*, of course – before the people he owed money to came banging on his door. In 59 BC, he left Spain just as quickly, to stand for the top job – the post of consul.

TO THE VERY TOP

By now, the famous Roman general, Pompey, had returned to Rome. He was a hero. He had defeated those troublesome pirates, conquered Asia, sent untold riches back to Rome and was a general all-round good guy. Cicero feared that Pompey might turn up at the head of a huge army but, instead, he arrived with wagonloads of treasure and a bunch of foreign princes (prisoners from the countries he'd invaded). He was greeted by thousands and thousands and thousands of excited people, and a monumental column was put up in Rome to commemorate his victories.

WHO'S THAT, THEN?

POMPEY

HE'S SMALLER THAN I IMAGINED

HE MUST HAVE A GOOD HEAD FOR HIGHTS!

PROBLEMS FOR POMPEY

Like Caesar, Pompey wanted to be consul but, unlike Caesar, he'd been consul once before. At that time there had to be a gap of ten years before you could hold the post again, so Pompey was disqualified. He also failed to pass a law that would give his soldiers land once they retired from the army. This was an embarrassing defeat, because Pompey wanted to repay his troops for the victories they'd helped him win. One of Pompey's major disadvantages was that he wasn't a very good public speaker.

CICERO SUCKS UP

Cicero, no longer consul, was looking for a strong and popular ally in the Senate, and Pompey seemed the obvious choice. He took Pompey's side in a number of debates and Pompey was so pleased that he called Cicero 'the saviour of the world', which was a bit over the top! Cicero, on the other hand, said that Pompey 'sits silent, admiring his fine clothes'!

YOU CAN'T HAVE BOTH

Now Caesar was on his way home to stand for consul in the elections. The trouble was that he'd also asked for a 'triumph' – not a British motor car but an official hero's welcome – after his successes in Spain. The rules stated that, if someone wanted a triumph, he couldn't enter the city of Rome until the date that had been fixed for it . . . and Caesar needed to be *in* Rome to whip up support for his election.

There were plenty of exceptions made to this rule so Caesar was sure that he'd only have to ask and he'd be allowed in now and get the victory parade later. Unfortunately, a man named Cato, who bitterly hated Caesar, had become very powerful in the Senate and made them vote against Caesar's request – perhaps he hoped to run for consul himself and thought that Caesar would settle for the triumph instead. In fact, Caesar said to forget the hero's welcome. It was the top job in the land he was after.

POMPEY AND CAESAR

Pompey and Caesar instantly got on well together. Caesar was the one person who'd supported Pompey throughout his entire absence, and Pompey had never forgotten how he and Metellus had stuck up for him when times were tough. Caesar clearly had the support of the people behind him, and Pompey had the support of the army. Now all they needed was the support of some of the *optimates*, and they'd have an unbeatable team.

THE FIRST TRIUMVIRATE

Caesar had a friend called Crassus, who represented the *optimates*, and he joined Caesar and Pompey's group, or *amicitia*. Now the three men headed a party that was just about ready to revolutionize Rome from within. This powerful new political force was known as the First Triumvirate. Caesar was eager for Cicero and the aristocracy to be a part of it too, but didn't have an important role to offer Cicero. So Cicero would have nothing to do with them and became a powerful enemy.

MORE MARRIAGES

The link between Caesar and Pompey was made even stronger when Pompey married Caesar's daughter, Julia. It was time for Julius Caesar to marry again too. His third wife was Calpurnia, a woman from a very well-to-do family. Her father, Calpurnius Piso – who became a consul the year after Caesar – was also a member of the triumvirate.

LOVELY COUPLE... WHICH OF THEM'S YOUR DAUGHTER?

VI VII VIII IX X

CONSUL AT LONG LAST

To the surprise of no one, Julius Caesar became consul and took up his new post at the beginning of 59 BC. Two consuls were always elected, and the power shared between them. Caesar's enemies, the *optimates*, made sure that the other consul was their man Marcus Bibulus, even though it did take a lot of bribing.

NO CONSOLATION PRIZE

Consuls ruled for a year, and the year was traditionally named after them. Julius Caesar was so much more powerful and impressive than his puppet co-consul Bibulus that the year 59 BC became jokingly referred to as the 'Year of the Consuls Julius and Caesar'. Bibulus's name didn't even get a look in!

PROMISES TO KEEP

One of Caesar's first acts was to try to pass the law granting lands to soldiers who'd fought for Rome – something which Pompey had tried and failed to do. When Bibulus and the *optimates* tried to prevent this, soldiers from Pompey's former legions rioted. They even broke Bibulus's seal of office in the commotion. Bibulus made a hasty retreat and looked out for any ill omens that might prove the gods were against Caesar's actions. The law was passed, and Pompey's men were happy at long last. Their service to their country had been repaid.

POWER TO THE PEOPLE!

As consul, Caesar was always careful to try to rule by the book. Whenever possible, he would try to get his new laws passed by the Senate . . . but, if this failed, he would turn to the People's Assembly. The aristocratic *optimates* hated the way that things were turning out – they'd never had such little power – but they were frightened of Julius Caesar's enormous support, so didn't dare act against him (in public, at least). For the very first time in the entire history of the Roman Republic, here was a government that really seemed to represent most ordinary citizens, instead of just the rich and powerful. This was unheard of! If that wasn't bad enough, Caesar was making sure that the workings of the Senate were made much more open to the public.

FOR THE GOOD OF THE PEOPLE

As consul, Caesar passed many popular laws: laws lowering the crippling taxes that rich farmers had to pay, laws protecting ordinary citizens against corruption and violence, laws against bribery at elections and laws against rulers in the provinces taking money for themselves rather than for Rome.

FROM CONSUL TO SOLDIER

Although Rome was still a republic – the Roman Empire, with a capital 'E' and ruled over by an emperor, was yet to come – it did have an empire (with a small 'e'), made up of lots of provinces under Roman rule. When Caesar's year as consul was over, he was appointed to Gaul. Here was a chance to gain further glory by winning great military battles abroad.

Caesar's father-in-law, Piso, was the new consul along

with an old friend of Pompey's, both of whom were great supporters of Caesar, so he felt that he was leaving Rome in safe hands. He might not be the most senior man in government any more, but he was the most important man in the First Triumvirate which was now the ruling party in Rome. The *optimates* were a thing of the past in the Republic.

CICERO DESTROYED

While Caesar made preparations to go to Gaul, he offered his old enemy Cicero the job as his second-in-command. Cicero was about to stand trial for having had those men accused of being 'traitors to Rome' executed without a fair trial, back in 62 BC – if you've no idea what I'm on about, look at page 32. Cicero refused Caesar's offer, convinced that he'd been such a popular consul in his own day that no one would find him guilty of anything.

Ooops! Deary, deary me. How wrong he was. He was found guilty, banished from Rome and told that if he came within four hundred miles of it he'd be put to death. His houses were burned and his property confiscated. He fled to Macedonia. And who had been behind Cicero's downfall? Who had led the trial against him? A man called Clodius, more famously remembered as 'Pretty Boy', who – disguised as a woman – had entered Caesar's home and caused him to divorce his second wife.

TO GAUL!

We know a great deal about the Gallic Wars – that's *Gallic* meaning 'of Gaul', not *garlic* which is something you wear around your neck to ward off vampires – because of Caesar's own reports. At the end of each year, he'd send a whole book full of information back to Rome. These were put together and became known as the *De Bello Gallico* – not to be confused with three later books called *De Bello Civili*, which he wrote about the civil war – and did a great deal to help build his reputation as a super, fab, brilliant general. He needed to stick in people's minds whilst he was away from home because he wanted to be re-elected as consul when he finally returned to Rome.

CAESAR, THE GENERAL

There's no doubt that Caesar really was an excellent general, at least as good as Pompey. He gained a reputation for his swift action and extreme patience . . . If he had to wait for an advantage, he'd wait but, if the time was right, he'd act in an instant. This meant that he, and not the enemy, nearly always got to choose where and when to fight. He built up very good intelligence reports of what the enemy force were up to, and always kept supply and communications lines open. With victory after victory, he defeated the Germans and suppressed the Belgian tribes in the North. Back in Rome, people were talking of Julius Caesar as the 'successor to Marius'. Here was a real hero!

WITH FRIENDS LIKE THESE

At home, Caesar's ally Pompey was far from thrilled by just what an amazing soldier Caesar had turned out to be. *He* was supposed to be the famous general, not Caesar! It wasn't fair! And Crassus, the third member of the First Triumvirate, wasn't getting on too well with Pompey now either. Then Caesar had reason to be annoyed with Pompey. Remember Caesar's old enemy Cicero, who was banished from Rome and told that if he came back within four hundred miles he'd be put to death? Well, Pompey had arranged for his return to Rome. Cicero was back.

MAKING TROUBLE ONCE MORE

Cicero was glad to be back and used what influence he had left from the old days to make sure that Pompey was given Rome's grain distribution rights for five years. Now, grain distribution rights might not sound very exciting – the sort of things you might be made to write an essay about at school as a punishment, in fact – but they were very important. They meant that Pompey could decide exactly who got what grain and when. The most important food in Rome was bread. Without it, people rioted or starved. The grain was used to make bread and Pompey now had control over the grain.

THE MEETING AT LUCA

In May 56 BC, Julius Caesar invited Pompey and Crassus to a place in Gaul called Luca to patch up their disagreements. It was important that their alliance kept control of power in Rome. They weren't the only ones at the meeting, though. As well as Roman governors from Sardinia and Spain, about two hundred senators turned up too! Today, this would be a bit like lots of members of the

British House of Commons having a meeting in France. It was unheard of!

AGREEMENT IS REACHED

The meeting agreed that Pompey and Crassus would be the consuls in 55 BC, while Caesar's command in Gaul would continue for another five years. Pompey would get to rule Spain for five years and Crassus would get Syria – they were dividing the world between them! On Caesar's return from Gaul, he would become consul for the second time - there were no more rules about having to wait ten years.

OFF TO FACE THE BRUTISH BRITS!

This decided, Caesar returned to battle and to more great victories. He crossed the River Rhine, defeated rebellious

German tribes, then sailed across the Channel to Britain in 55 BC, with about 10,000 soldiers from two legions. At what we now call the white cliffs of Dover, he was greeted by rows of frightening-looking painted warriors, jeering at them from the cliff tops, ready to throw rocks and spears down on his soldiers the minute they stepped ashore. Caesar decided that it was probably best not to land there, and took the fleet further along the coast. He found a beach just as the British warriors swarmed down onto it with their horses and weapons.

IN DEEP WATER

Caesar's forces anchored their ships off shore (where the water was still up to their necks) and wondered what to do next. These hairy blue Brits looked far from friendly . . . They were blue because they'd covered themselves in woad – a blue dye made from plants – to make themselves look even more frightening. Unlike the half-naked natives, the invading Romans were wearing heavy armour and weren't

too keen on wading ashore, especially to be met by this not so welcoming bunch of folk.

DEFEND THE EAGLE!

Caesar then sent the ships carrying his archers nearer the shore, so that they could ward off the Britons with a shower of arrows. The officer who carried the silver eagle – the symbol of the Tenth Legion of Roman soldiers which had come with Caesar – then leapt into the water. The others then followed him, with a cheer. The defending Britons rode their horses into the water to face the invaders and managed to hold them back for a while. Once on land, however, the Roman soldiers could use their superior weapons and training. The Britons rode off and the Romans set up camp.

FLOAT ON

The Britons soon agreed peace with the Romans, until a spring tide came along and washed many of Caesar's moored ships and much of his equipment off the beach. The Britons then attacked . . . were easily defeated, and asked for peace again! Caesar decided that it was a good idea for him and his troops to head back to the Continent.

BACK IN FORCE

Caesar returned to Britain on 21 July of the following year (54 BC) with five legions and 800 boats and ships. They landed at Deal, where a camp was set up, guarded by about 6,000 Romans! The fleet of ships stayed anchored off shore. Horrified by the size of the invaders' army, the Britons had fled inland. Some stood and fought at a river crossing, but were soon forced back into the forests.

THAT SINKING FEELING

Caesar and his men were about to launch an all-out attack on the Britons when news reached him from Deal that a gale had wrecked his entire fleet. His ships and boats lay smashed to pieces on the beach. Caesar ordered his army to halt their advance and he returned to Deal. He quickly realized that only forty or so of his ships were damaged beyond repair. The rest could be saved. He soon organized the repair work and was back with his army in a week.

AN ADMIRABLE FOE

Caesar stated in his writings that the Britons were brave warriors and fought well, but they were members of different tribes and didn't fight together as one force. More skirmishes followed. In the end, some of the defeated tribes agreed to send regular payments to Rome. Satisfied with this, Caesar and his force went home, with thousands of British prisoners to use as slaves. Caesar's expedition to Britain made him more famous still. He was the first Roman to visit this strange land. The Romans neither conquered nor settled in Britain until almost a hundred years after that.

VENI, VIDI, VICI

Julius Caesar wasn't just a great soldier, he was great at promoting himself too. After one of his many victories abroad he's supposed to have said 'I came, I saw, I conquered', which is a pretty good line anyway but, in Latin, it's even better. It's: 'Veni, vidi, vici.' Latin is a dead language (which means that Latin scholars are the only people to speak it), so no one is sure how words were pronounced. Some brainboxes think that the 'v's were spoken like 'w's, so 'Veni, vidi, vici' would be pronounced 'Weni, widi, wici.'

UNREST IN ROME

With the Senate and army's attention turned to troubles abroad – and, boy, were there plenty of them – times were tough in Rome, where the mobs seemed to rule the streets. Ordinary people were desperate for law and order but violence and corruption made elections impossible. By 54

BC there was talk of making Pompey a dictator with emergency powers to control the crisis. Then, in 53 BC, the third member of the First Triumvirate, Crassus, died in battle. The original alliance was now crumbling.

EXTREME MEASURES

Much to the *optimates*' disappointment, Caesar and Pompey remained loyal to each other for the time being. Pompey was happy to raise three legions for Caesar's campaign against the Gauls in 53 BC. When, in January 52 BC, Clodius – Pretty Boy, remember? – was murdered by a group of armed *optimates*, led by a man name Titus

Annius Milo, there were riots . . . and, during those riots, the Senate house was burnt to the ground! Pompey was hurriedly elected as sole consul, with a mission to sort the whole mess out.

POMPEY'S POWER GROWS

Being consul on your own was unheard of. There were always *two* consuls. So Pompey made it clear that he would choose a fellow consul and many people expected this to be Julius Caesar. They were wrong. Pompey chose a man named Metellus Scipio, who was strongly suspected of bribery and corruption and was a friend of the murderous Titus Annius Milo! Pompey also married Scipio's daughter, his wife Julia (Caesar's daughter) having died.

THE SNEAKY SENATE

52 BC to 50 BC was a time of revolts. The Gauls had found themselves a leader to unite under; a man called Vercingetorix. Caesar spent his time in battle after battle, defeating the enemies of Rome. He ruled by terror. If having prisoners' hands chopped off would make them take him seriously, he'd have their hands chopped off.

The now-hostile Senate had rather hoped that Caesar would be killed fighting . . . it would have made life a lot simpler. But in the spring of 50 BC, he returned to the provinces he governed. A supporter of Caesar's was then elected as consul in 49 BC – at least, he had by far the most votes. But somehow, these were discounted and two other men got the job! It seemed to be the new consuls' ambition in life to make sure that Caesar didn't receive any recognition or reward for his great victories abroad. It had been agreed that Caesar would be consul in 48 BC, but they'd do everything in their powers to stop this.

POMPEY, THE ENEMY

Jealous of Caesar's incredible power and popularity in the provinces, and pleased with his own ever-growing importance in Rome, Pompey now decided to try to destroy his one-time friend. Through the Senate, he ordered that Caesar give up his position and return to Rome. If he didn't resign and disband his army, he would be considered an enemy of the Republic. Caesar still had support in the Senate from representatives of the people called the 'Tributes of the People'. They had the power to throw out the order, which they did. Unfortunately, the Senate then went and threw *them* out!

BATTLE LINES ARE DRAWN

Pompey had more troops than Caesar but they were dotted all over the place and those he had nearby weren't 'battle ready'. Caesar, on the other hand, had thousands of troops who were ready, willing and very able. It was time to make a stand.

Early in 49 BC, Julius Caesar and his armies crossed the river Rubicon which divided Gaul and what we now call Italy. It is then that he is supposed to have said *'alea iacta est'*, which is the Latin for 'the die is cast'. In other words, this was one big moment in history with no turning back . . . He was about to take control of Rome.

FLEE! FLEE!

The Senate panicked and left Rome . . . In fact, they left Italy altogether, ending up in what is now Albania, and so did Pompey. No one wanted to face Caesar with his vast army of well-trained, battle seasoned soldiers. When Caesar arrived in Rome, he was delighted to find that his enemies had left in such a hurry that they'd left all the money in the Treasury! He could now set up his own Senate and had the money to run the government.

FACING THE ENEMY

Caesar put a politician and soldier called Mark Antony in charge of the legions in Italy, while he went off to Spain and crushed Pompey's supporters. (Most of them did the sensible thing and switched sides, becoming loyal to Caesar.) He then returned to Rome. Meanwhile, Pompey raised an enormous army in Macedonia and was ready for action. Caesar's forces went to face him, but were badly outnumbered. Soon, Mark Antony and his troops joined Caesar, but still Pompey didn't attack. For some strange reason, Pompey then withdrew his forces (which is a bit like retreating, but before any fighting has actually taken place).

WINNER ALL THE WAY

Caesar was puzzled by Pompey's actions. He said, 'Today the enemy would have won if they were commanded by a winner'. Caesar was the winner, though. At a place called Pharsalus, his 32,000 men faced Pompey's 43,000 and, in the largest battle in the Roman civil war, defeated them. He was kind to the defeated armies, pardoning the troops — something most unusual in those days. More battles were to follow, but Caesar was now undisputed ruler of Rome . . . while all Pompey could do was flee to Egypt with his family.

DEATH ON THE SANDS

Arriving at Egypt, poor old Pompey was killed before he'd had time to get off the boat and up the beach! He was murdered by his own men. Caesar arrived in Egypt not long after him, and became involved in Egyptian politics. In the city of Alexandria, there was some dispute over whether an Egyptian queen, named Cleopatra, could rule alongside her brother Ptolemy. Caesar decreed that she should, and soon rumours spread that the two were lovers.

CAESAR AND CLEOPATRA

It seems more than likely that Caesar did, indeed, find Cleopatra charming and that he let this influence what he did . . . but the old *optimates* in Rome blew everything out of proportion, claiming that this was the love affair of the century. Cleopatra certainly played up the story for all it was worth – she was only sixteen when she met Caesar – and even claimed that Caesar was the father of a boy she named Caesarion. Unluckily for poor old Caesarion, it was later proved that he was an impostor and he was put to death. (Cleopatra became Mark Antony's girlfriend after Caesar died.)

THE EGYPTIANS ATTACK

The Egyptian city of Alexandria was a huge, sprawling place full of everyone from pirates to ex-Roman soldiers . . . and they came after Caesar. The Egyptians were excellent sailors, so Caesar was quick to put their ships out of action by setting fire to the docks and seizing the Pharos lighthouse and the strip connecting it to the mainland. He then fortified the palace and surrounding houses, for him and his troops to hole up in, and defended the harbour against the enemy.

WATER, WATER EVERYWHERE

The Egyptians flooded the palace's fresh water supply with sea water, so that Caesar and his men would have nothing to drink. But new wells were dug and fresh water found. The Egyptians then rushed the harbour and tried to regain it, forcing Caesar to abandon a ship he was on board at the time. According to some very unlikely versions of events he had to swim to safety carrying his manuscript for his books on the civil war! The fighting dragged on but, finally, Caesar was victorious.

AND, LOOK. IT'S EVEN GOT A NICE LITTLE HANDLE TO WINCH UP THE BUCKET.

IT'S LOVELY!

PROMISES TO KEEP

Soldiers of the Tenth Legion demanded to see Caesar when they learnt that they were now being sent to Africa, instead of being allowed to retire peacefully as promised. When Caesar appeared he didn't call them 'brothers-in-arms' as he had done before, but 'citizens' which meant they were now freed from army duty. He gave them land too, saying, 'Never let it be said that I used you when in danger but was ungrateful when the perils had passed.' The men were so moved that they all pledged to remain soldiers and follow Caesar wherever he wanted them to go.

A TRIUMPHANT RETURN!

Having conquered Egypt, Caesar returned to Rome with Queen Cleopatra. All things Egyptian became very popular, and Caesar even took to dressing like one, which upset some important Romans! Having suppressed a few more rebellions here and there, Julius Caesar then held four separate triumph victory parades for himself in 46 BC (after all, he thought he deserved them). At the end of the final parade, he had Vercingetorix, the Gallic leader, strangled to add to the fun. Caesar was named dictator for the next ten years.

ABSOLUTE POWER

Still wildly popular with ordinary people, Caesar was offered the title of 'king' in 44 BC. At the time, he and Mark

Antony were the consuls. There had been kings before the Republic, but that had been a long time ago. Caesar declined the offer, and settled for being dictator *for life* instead. It wasn't that he didn't think he was worthy of being king. Far from it. As it was, he announced that he was descended from the legendary twins Romulus and Remus and set up his own religious cult, letting it be known that he was a god!

BEWARE THE IDES OF MARCH

Unfortunately for Julius Caesar, his days were numbered. A man with so much power was bound to have powerful enemies. Many people thought that he'd got too big for his boots . . . well, his open-toed sandals! After a rousing speech in Caesar's favour from Cicero – yes, he was *still* around – the *optimates* had sworn loyalty to Caesar, who came to the

Senate, unarmed, every day ... But there were those plotting his downfall. Despite 'bad omens' that he should be beware the ides of March – 'ides' simply means the 15th – it was business as usual for Caesar that day ... until he was stabbed by a number of conspirators, including his friend Brutus (whom, you may remember, some claim was his son).

THE DEATH OF CAESAR

Caesar is famous for saying '*Et tu, Brute?*' when he died, meaning 'You too, Brutus?', but reliable eyewitness accounts suggest that he actually said nothing. His enemies – most of whom were so-called 'friends' – stabbed him twenty-seven times and each other a few times in their eagerness to do the job. Cicero witnessed the attack. Those who killed Caesar claimed that he was a tyrant and that what they did was for the liberty and good of Rome. What followed was seventeen bloody years of civil war.

THE NAME LIVES ON

Julius Caesar had such a big impact on world history that his very name became an important title. Not only did later rulers of Rome call themselves 'Caesar', but the Russian word 'Czar' and the German word 'Kaiser' also come from Caesar's name . . . Today, the title of 'Caesar' is tied up with so many important Roman rulers, it's easy to forget that it all dates back to this one extraordinary man, murdered by his own countrymen. The first man to hold Caesar's name as a title was his own niece's son Octavian. Octavian changed his name to Caesar Augustus when the Roman Republic became the Roman Empire (with that capital 'E') and he became its first emperor in 27 BC.

TIMELINE,

at home and abroad

*c.*100BC	Julius Caesar is born. *Temple of the Sun, Teotihuacan,* *built in ancient Mexico.* *Syrians invent glass-blowing.* *Piston bellows invented in China.* *Water-powered mills used for* *grinding corn in Albania.*
73 – 71 BC	Spartacus's slave revolt (defeated).
60 BC	*The Roman poet Lucretius writes six* *books on the idea that* *everything is made up of* *tiny atoms.*
58 – 51 BC	Caesar's Gallic Wars.
51 BC	Cleopatra becomes last queen of Egypt.
48 BC	Caesar defeats Pompey.
47 BC	*Great Library at Alexandria burns* *down.* Pompey murdered.
44 BC	Caesar stabbed to death by Brutus and chums.